Loretta Santini

CAPRI
magic

Published and printed by

NARNI - TERNI

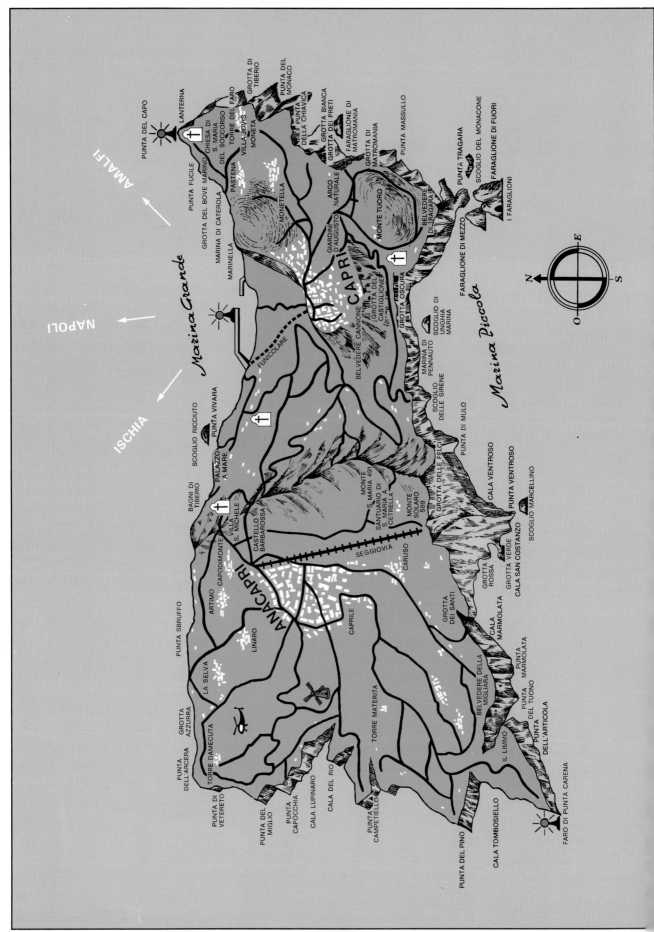

CAPRI

The island of Capri, a geographical prolongation of the Sorrento Peninsula, closes the Bay of Naples to the South, just as the island of Ischia, to the North, gave a foretaste of the beauties of this part of Italy. Thus Capri embraces the marvels of this stretch of coast and faces the no less picturesque landscape of the Bay of Salerno.

It is a small island, covering barely 10 square Km., and is roughly quadrangular in shape. One is immediately struck by the cliffs rising sheer out of the sea, the luxurious vegetation covering most of the island, and the dazzling white houses scattered among the green.

The little town of Capri is the main centre. To the West of it stands Anacapri, on a high plateau on the slopes of Monte Solaro. Most of the inhabitants live in these two places. The fishermen's families for the most part live at Marina Grande, which is also the island's main port, while Marina Piccola, situated on the South coast, is a very popular little resort with a marvellous position.

Naturally, tourism is the main business of the island's inhabitants, but some of the people are engaged in fishing and the cultivation of olives and the vine. The island's flora and fauna (especially as regards fish), are particularly interesting and varied. The flora above all, thanks to the large number of species it offers, is a valuable asset to the island, forming part of its many beauties.

To list the beauties that have made Capri famous throughout the world, would only mean making a dry enumeration without being able to catch its spirit. Capri is a jewel box full of marvels, and this is due above all to Nature. The Blue Grotto, the Faraglioni, the Natural Arch, the countless other grottoes scattered along its coast and the steep cliffs falling sheer into the sea, are only a few of its best known features. In addition, there are the magnificent views, the picturesque depths with the crystal clear water, the many parks and public gardens, the characteristic architecture of the houses, and the local colour that can be noted in the buildings and the products of handicraft. Nor should one overlook the interesting remains of Roman times, such as those of the splendid Villa Jovis, or the Villa Damecuta, and the beautiful Villa San Michele dating from the early years of this century.

Capri has been rightly called the Pearl of the Sea: to know it means to rediscover the creative force of Nature and the sense of its beauty.

Marina Grande

The Marina Grande is the ancient port of Capri and its only important landing place, owing to the islands particular morphology with cliffs falling sheer to the sea all around its coastline. The other landing place (though not the main one) is situated on the South coast of the island, where the attractive little resort of Marina Piccola is situated.

Marina Grande is well equipped to accomodate private yachts and the countless regular services which bring thousands upon thousands of tourists here every year from the various harbours of the Bay of Naples.

The village of Marina Grande stands all along the Bay of Capri, with its row of typical and attractive fishermen's cottages, huddling one on top of another, almost in a single mass and distinguishable only by their bright, varied colours. From Marina Grande a road leads to the little town of Capri and other places on the island, and there is a funicular that starts here and goes straight up to Capri. A regular service of boats goes from the port to the Blue Grotto.

Let us take a last look at the island as a whole before going up to Capri and Anacapri. From the harbour of Marina Grande can be seen rising up the two high rocky spurs, above which there are two small plateaus. To the West, in the line of Monte Solaro, stands Anacapri, to the East Monte Tiberio. Capri lies in the little valley between the two peaks, nestling on the slopes of Monte Tiberio. A dense vegetation covers all the lower part of the island, while higher up the rock rises steep and bare; at other points it falls sheer to the sea, creating inlets, grottoes and most picturesque corners.

The road which starts from Marina Grande leads up to the centre of Capri in a series of steep twists and turns.

Before venturing into the characteristic narrow lanes of the little town, the visitor's gaze can roam over the Marina Grande beneath, and the coast of Sorrento in the distance. It is a truly breath-taking view, but other, still finer, ones await us. The inhabitants call this Belvedere the « little balcony », for this is what it looks like. It is situated in the oper space at the terminus of the funicular railway.

PIAZZA UMBERTO I (THE PIAZZET-
TA) — One side of the Piazzetta is
taken up by the Church of Santo
Stefano. In front of it there is a
wide flight of steps, where tourists
are wont to sit, to rest and enjoy
the busy life of the Piazzetta and
the mild air of the island. The
church, in a local version of the
Baroque style, stands on the site
of the ancient Cathedral. It was
rebuilt several times, and contains
valuable works of art, of which the
fine polychrome marble floor de-
serves particular mention.

The St. Stefano-Church

General view

Corso Vittorio Emanuele

The Certosa San Giacomo
(Monastery of St James)

Erected in 1371-74 by Count Giacomo Arcucci, feudal lord of the island, the charterhouse of S. Giacomo, remains inspite of numerous reconstructions, the most important example of that Caprese architecture which slowly maturing midst the ruins of Roman villas found in the oldest churches and the monumental Certosa ist truest creations thansk to local craftsmen faithful to the Roman tradition.
The domed roofs of the house and churches provide a harmonious and rational harmony with nature. Castles, churches and houses weave together with the ruins of the roman villas a modulated consonance of volumes, forms and colours in the Caprese countryside.
Thus from the imperial villa on Mount Tiberius to the majestic charterhouse between the heights of Tuoro and Castiglione opposite the Faraglioni, the passage from the imperial hermitage to the monastic hermitage seems obvions and natural.
The Certosa was not only the ideal place for the ascetic life of the monks but was also an economic force on the island with possessions extending here and there and even around Naples.
Devastated by pirates during the 16th century the charterhouse was restored by the monks who erected a defensive tower which collapsed in 1808.
Following disagreements between the regular clergy and the secular clergy the charterhouse was supressed in 1807 by Giuseppe Bonaparte and thereafter had various uses.
Partially restored, the monumental construction includes the church and convent which enclose a small 14th century cloister dominated by the baroque clocktower and the late 16th century cloister.

The large cloister (photo the side) is surrounded by a pillared portico around which are grouped the cells, dispensary, capitulary, garden and other rooms. To the right on the cliff eage is the Prior's quarters isolated from the rest of the Convent and probably constructed in the 16th century.

Of considerable interest is the Church which has anogical portal decorated with base relief figures of St. Bruno and St. Giacomo and a 13th century fresco. The inside, photo on the opposite page has only one nave and the vault and cross-vault characteristic to Caprese architecture.

Unfortunately little remains of the 16th century frescos.

In the photos on this page we can admire some of the statues corroded by sea water which have been found on the sea bottom of the Blue Grotto and which are today kept in the courtyard of the Certosa of San Giacomo.
One hypothesis is that these statues prove that during the time of Augustus and Tiberius the grotto was a nymphaea and the remains of mural works now submerged show just how much the Grotto has dropped in level since Roman times.

The Cannon-Belvedere and Faraglioni

The Faraglioni - Panoramic foreshortening

THE PARK OF AUGUSTUS and the FARAGLIONI — This is one of the most picturesque places of Capri; it is a public garden with a wealth of various plants, criss-crossed by paths, lanes and steps leading to the various view-points, from which can be seen the Southern part of the island, the MARINA PICCOLA below, and above all, the famous FARAGLIONI, emerging like rocky little islands from the deep blue water.

Via Krupp ➤

Marina Piccola

The Faraglioni

Panoramic view: Capri and the harbour, Sorrento's peninsula and the Faraglioni rocks

The Natural Arch

The particular kind of rock in the island (limestone) has given rise to some fantastic shapes. External agents, such as wind and rain, operating for centuries on these rocky cliffs, have transformed the appearance of the rock faces, creating fantastic and sometimes daring shapes, as for instance the so-called NATURAL ARCH. There is also an interesting natural cave, the Grotta di Matromania, used by the ancient Romans for the worship of Cybele (here are found interesting remains of mosaic decorations and masonry).

The Grotta di Matromania

Marina Piccola

This is the other landing place (after Marina Grande) of which the island can boast. Well equipped, and favoured by the special advantages of its surroundings, it is one of the most popular and sought-after holiday resorts, a refined and luxurious bathing place.

The Marina Piccola bay

arina Piccola and the bathing beaches

Villa Jovis

Inhabited since prehistoric times as shown by weapons and implements found, part of the Greek colonies first and later Roman, it was in 29 AD that Capri passed from its solitary existence as a small island to the centre of Imperial Roman life.

It was in that year that Ottaviano (not yet Augustus) sailing towards Naples was attracted by the soaring cliffs and the gigantic peaks of the Faraglioni. He landed at Capri and so delightful was his stay that he did not hestiate to withdraw the island from Naple's domain and make it part of the growing principality.

Ottaviano almost up to his death in 14 AD frequently stayed in Capri and after his death Tiberius made Capri an imperial residence.

However where Augustus serenly loved Capri, Tiberius, old and misanthopist that he was was a splendid and jealous lover and from this morbid love and his bitter delight of ex-ile and solitude comes the myth of Tiberius, a legend which even today gives life to the deserted ruins of the palazzi and roman villas of Capri.

Mythic even is the number of 12 villas which, according to Tacito, the emporer had built on the island, the same number as the twelve divinities of Olympus. Unfortunately, owing to rearrangements made through the centuries, it is no longer possible to control the number of the villas and their sites. Only three have been verified and indeed excel for their grandiose structure and the vast area they cover: one on the Damecuta plain, a second known as « Palazzo on the Sea » with a descent which leads to the Tiberius Baths and finally the third, Villa Jovis (photo the side) crowns the eastern headland of the island where Jupiter and his earthly pontiff Tiberius could surround themselves with threatening and brilliant splendour. Villa Jovis the largest and best conserved of the island's imperial villas unites historical interest and the singular beauty of the site. Near the entrance to the excavations is the so-called « Tiberius' Jump », a frightening rocky precipice 297 metres above the sea, from where according to tradition Tiberius forced his victims to leap.

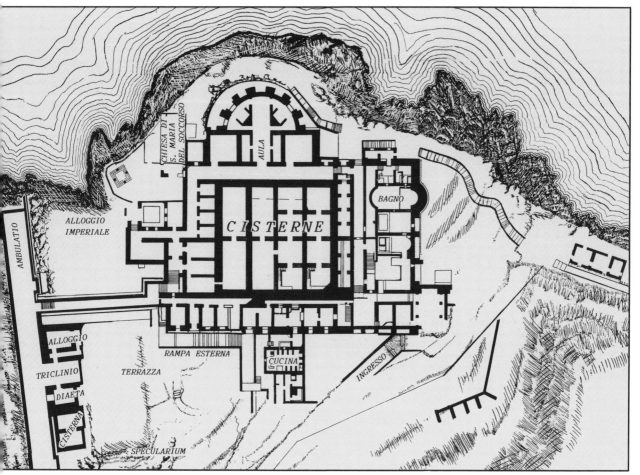

Villa Jovis, particulars of which can be seen in these photographs, was the favourite residence of Tiberius who stayed on the island for the last ten years of his life (37 - 26 AD) with a small following and administered the Empire from here. This was the most splendid period in the ancient history of Capri inspite of the fame of Tiberius' perversity. Indeed that after Tiberius' death the Senate ordered all his villas on Capri to be demolished is merely a legend.

The island infact continued to be frequented by successive emporers and Roman aristocrats and the important garrison established in Tiberius' time to protect him remained.

Remembered by both Svetonio and Plinius, the Villa covers the summit of Mount Tiberius with an area of 7000 square ma-

teres. With woods, gardens and nympheae the area covered must have been greater still. The building with floors and terraces connected by stairways extends from Torre del Faro, probably of the Tiberian era, to the summit of the promontory.

The various quarters are centred around a square area which has four cisterns carved in the rock to collect rain water. To the north is a large panoramic terrace probably the most grandiose part of the original structure.

Looted during the first excavations in Borvon timesfi stripped of its marble floors and tampered with in the course of the centuries, the villa was first explored in 1827. Only in 1932 and 1935 A. Maiuri completed the excavations which brought this splendid villa fully to light - a villa of the first half of the Empire.

Capri is the island of natural beauties, as can be seen from the many grottoes scattered around its coast, with their varied and picturesque formations.
The photograph shows views of the Faraglioni.

Monacone Reef

Masullo Promontory and Villa Malaparte

The Blue Grotto

A high rocky spur which extends in a sea of blue, cliffs to which cling trees twisted by the wind into the strangest forms, tiny roads with white walls which lead to little houses wither still, a square crowded night and day with the life which elsewhere seems hidden, modern hotels, shops, the crowd with famous names, strangely dressed figures and simple folk. Capri is this and more, few places in Italy have so many faces so different and varied grouped together in such a small space as Capri.

The island owes its worldwide fame to the splendid natural beauty, the ancient wyths and legends, the fascinating remains of imperial villas, the characteristic domes of the houses and churches but most of all to the famous marine cathedral that is the Blue Grotto.

This ancient cave in the northern coast of the island, made larger by landslides and lowered by the effect of bradysism so as to be partially under sea level owes its fame to particular its geological conditions. The tiny entrance only two meters wide and one metre high means that the grotto receives light which has passed underwater. This light freed from the water colours the walls, roof and stalactites an intense blue. The light makes the water opalescent and anything submerged in the water appears silver.

Celebrated as one of the wonders of our coast, the grotto was known to the ancients as hàs been shown from the Roman remains found both inside and outside the groto. Tiberius probably transformed the grotto into a nymphea, a sort of temple dedicated to marine gods. It was easily reached from Villa di Gradola the ruins of which are above the grotto. In time the existence of the grotto as forgotten even though the inhabitants of Capri knew of it before Angelo Ferraro's visit on 16th May 1822 and indeed visited the grotto before the apparent discovery by the poet Augusto Kopish of Breslavia and his friends on 17th August 1826. In any case it was at this time that the grotto made its official entrance in the list of natural wonders of Capri and began with its magic colour to increase the fame of Capri.

Thus the myth of the sirens has returned to where it was born, in the sea in the recesses of a magic cliff which men can enter through a narrow fissure and find the magic spectacle of the grotto. Once inside looking down in the crystal water to the tiny pebbles at the bottom or looking around at the blue rock wrapped in an enchanted light it is possible to discover the secret fascination that is Capri.

The road that led from Marina Grande to Capri, now goes up to the other little town on the island, Anacapri. All the way, the road cut into the rock climbs up steeply and one has a continuous succession of marvellous views: the eye ranges not only over Capri and Marina Grande, but embraces in the distance the coastline of Sorrento. At the top, from the parapet at a height of some 300 metres above sea level, we are met by the extraordinary sight of the sheer wall of rock plunging down into the sea. It is a truly impressive sight.

Anacapri

Anacapri is the second town on the island after Capri. It stands on the slopes of Monte Solaro, 275 metres above sea level, a level piece of ground, which is particularly rich in natural and cultivated vegetation (olive groves, vineyards). The rocks and the luxuriant greenery make it an attractive place, popular with those visitors who seek a quiet and restful holiday on the island.

Anacapri is a high class holiday centre which attracts crowds of visitors every year, thanks aso to the quality and efficiency of the accommodation it offers. There are many shops and popular boutiques, and hee too, one finds the characteristic stalls in a row all along the edge of the road, striking a homely note among the luxurious hotels, restaurants and cafés. Anacapri is also the best starling point for excursions to Monte Solaro, and also for visiting the famous Villa San Michele, the Imperial Roman Villa and the Blue Grotto.

Via Orlandi and the Piazza della Vittoria form the centre of Anacapri. The parish church of Santa Sofia and the Caprile quarter around the little square of the same name, are also worth a visit.

Villa San Michele

VILLA SAN MICHELE — The photographs show: a general view of Capri from the Villa; the Museum and the Phoenician Steps. The latter consist of 881 steps climbing from Marina Grande to Villa San Michele and up to the Castello Barbarossa beyond it. Although known as the Phoenician Steps, they were made in ancient times by the Greeks, for whom they were the only means of access to this part of the island.

VILLA SAN MICHELE — This i
« must » for all who visit Ca
It was built on the remains o
Roman villa (some parts of wh
can still be seen inside), by
Swedish writer and physician A
Munthe, who lived here for so
40 years. He was the author
« The Story of San Michele » (a
which the Villa was called), wh
became a best-seller and v
translated into a great number
languages.

VILLA SAN MICHELE — The large villa is especially interesting for its 17th century furniture. There are also, as already mentioned, statues, columns and other Roman remains, found in the Roman building which previously stood on this spot, giving the place an air of discreet elegance.
On the right: the floor of majolica tiles in the Church of San Michele (1761).

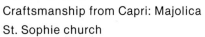

Craftsmanship from Capri: Majolica
St. Sophie church

St. Sophie church - The Turret-clock

The imperial villa of Damecuta

This is one of the villas which tradition says were built by the emperor Tiberius on the isle of Capri. If the ruins are anything to go by, then it must have been at least as grandiose as the Villa Jovis, because its certainly similar in style. Excavation work has brought to light a long loggia which must have served both as a panoramic terrace and as a place to relax or take a stroll. It's position is spectacular: poised on the high, rocky walls that fall away sheer to the sea below. Like the Villa Jovis, it too incorporates a series of cisterns for the preservation of fresh water.

This villa too was once rich in works of art — all of which have disappeared over the centuries.

The imperial residence was probably abandoned in the 1st century AD when the whole structure was covered in volcanic ash following the eruption of Vesuvius. The most interesting parts of the ruins that are visible, include the loggia, afore-mentioned, the residential quarters, the opus reticulatum, and the remains of a few columns.

There are other Roman ruins nearby, including the remains of a huge cistern which was adapted to other use in the Middle Ages.

The Barbarossa castle

The watch-Tower

Phoenix-Stairs and St. Antonio-church

The ancient fortress

Anacapri is the starting place for the excursion to Monte Solaro (589 metres), an excursion the tourist should not miss if he wishes to know the whole of Capri, and get a complete view of the island from the highest point.

The top can be reached on foot by way of Via San Michele (only recommended by good walkers), or by the chair-lift, which has its Lower Station in Piazza della Vittoria at Anacapri.

The chair-lift glides over woods and clearings, reaching the top of the mountain in about 15 minutes.

Here we are 589 metres above sea level; the island is stretched out below. We can recognise its shape and its various points, ranging with the eye over the manifold beauties of this rock which rises from the sea: all around us lies this little world where luxuriant nature reigns supreme. Near the summits is the 14th century Sanctuary of Santa Maria di Cetrella.

Capri view from Sorrento's peninsula

A few general views from the summit of Monte Solaro:
Marina Piccola and the Faraglioni, and the Punta del Faro,
or Punta Carena.

Europa Palace Hotel is the only Hotel Center with rooms and private Swimmingpools. Congress and Meeting-Center.

The lighthouse, a large red building, stands on the Carena Point on the extreme south-west of the island.

Inspite of roads and increasing traffic, Capri is one of the few places left where old mule tracks and paths allow visitors to enjoy on foot the natural beauty of the island. Anybody who thinks he can get to know the island visiting it in a car is illuding himself.

The tourist should visit the island on foot to appreciate it in full, a little like the drinker who sips his wine so as to enjoy the flavour a perfume, in this way the visitor will discover the most fascinating if less obvious aspects of this island.

Capri today is one of the best equipped intenational tourist resorts. A far cry from the time when an adventurous boat trip from Naples ended with simple homely hospitality of the locals as was the case for the first 18th century travellers who made Capri famous all over Europe.

Since then the tourist facilities have developed into a thriving modern industry with countless hotels, sporting and bathing facilities and nightclubs. Communications with Naples are now easy and comfortable with frequent boat trips or hydrofoils which bring the numerous tourists from the mainland to Capri.

One of the most enchanting and extraordinary aspects of Capri is the natural architecture of the coast with its variety of form and colour and the numerous grottos at sea level with their fabulous phosphorescent light. The sea has modelled and erroded these bizare caverns, roars in the dark recesses, laps against the encrusted walls and filters the blue light. Each and every grotto has a particular characteristic for which it is famous: The Green Grotto for example (once called the Turk's Grotto) has water of a brilliant emerald green. The Marvellous Grotto owes it name to the marvellous stalagmites. The Arsenal Grotto is of particular interest because it was mistakenly believed to have been a naval shipyard but was in reality a roman nymphaea as shown by the podium and coloured marbles found.

◄ The Coral Grotto

The White Grotto and the Marvellous Grotto ➤

The Green Grotto

INDEX

Photographs by:
Archivio Plurigraf
Archivio Interdipress
Foto Massimo Amendola - Amalfi
Foto aeree: Concess.
S.M.A. 240 - 263 - 587